Success is a System

Stan Peake

Praise for "Success is a System"

"Stan along with his 4th book *Success is a System* has created a book for anyone who looks in the mirror each day and demands more from themselves" - Nick Roud, Executive and Career Coach, New Zealand

"What I like about this book is that it is designed to be read in snippets or devoured all at once. Stan gives the reader just enough, at any one time, to enable them to understand how each piece can benefit their individual lives."
— Ben Baker, bestselling author, consultant and speaker, Vancouver, BC

"Stan has done it again, his ability to motivate through story-telling won't give you the opportunity to put this one down. My eyes are open, now I know that success truly is a system!" - Jonathan McCollin, Singer/songwriter, Cofounder, Griid, Toronto

"Identifying and achieving goals that make a difference is a journey of intention, resilience and practicality. This book provides a 360 degree view of key components for combining one's purpose, passion and potential to yield success." - Kalpana Shanmugham, PhD, Leadership/ Organizational Consultant & Coach, Atlanta, GA

"This is a precise, insightful, well written system for any leader who wants to check in and reflect regularly to get their mojo working. Stan has put together a powerful collection of thought provoking instructional chapters to get you to…. and keep you at the top of your game. This book should be a part of your business and personal leadership journey." - Gary Bertwistle, 3x TEC speaker of the year, bestselling author, host *The Mojo Radio Show* podcast, Sydney, Australia

"Stan has written a beautiful book from his heart that clearly reflects his philosophy that success in life, business, relationships is based on a system that we can all develop and improve daily. Stan uses many great examples and stories to illustrate his powerful messages…this book is a must-read for anyone and everyone who wants to achieve more and help others achieve more in their lives"!

- John Mattone, #1 executive coach in the world 2019, former coach to Steve Jobs, Orlando, FL

Dedication

This book is dedicated to the bold. The unconventional. To those who smile, even if imperceptibly, when they are told it can't be done, because they know *they will*. This book is written for you rebel, because it is who I am, it is who I admire, and it is who will change the world.

My aim is that the tools, habits, and attitudes described herein may become ammo in your war against complacency and in the struggle upstream against a plain existence.

Forward

As you will read in the following pages, success means different things to different people. Furthermore, my goal in writing this book is to help as many people as possible enhance their lives in some way. No two people are at the same point on the same journey at the same time. For these reasons, this book is meant to be digested and implemented as it lands for you on any given day.

You may well find that a second read leads to different insights and thus different benefit. Though there are clear suggestions and tools herein, this book is much more likely to work as a self-guided personal improvement toolbox than a step-by-step 'implement as is' checklist.

The book is organized starting from purpose and values as the ideological foundation of all that we do. From there, the focus shifts to mindset and attitude, and eventually to more tangible topics such as habits, relationships, ways to be more effective every day, and ways to give back and help others, because we all have something we can give.

Read it, may it resonate with you, and may you reap the rewards of whatever philosophies, strategies, and habits resonate with you!

Table of Contents

Purpose..10

Values..15

Mindset..21

Habits..40

Goal Setting..49

Effectiveness..54

Health...63

Relationships...69

Paying it Forward..76

Epilogue..82

Purpose

Purpose Ignites Strategy

If strategy is to goal as roadmap is to destination, then the only missing component is relevance. It is our purpose that adds conviction to our strategies, thereby ensuring their execution. In keeping with the roadmap analogy, this is the difference between driving to the store to get groceries, or driving to the airport to pick up a best friend you haven't seen in years (they're both errands, aren't they; yet you'd be infinitely more excited about the latter).

When you *find* your purpose, you *lose* your ability to quit.

Why Before How

As Peter Drucker, the father of modern management theory, cites, "nothing is more wasteful than making more efficient that which shouldn't be done in the first place". So often in life and in business we race to solve problems that don't even need an answer. Always ask "why is this important?" (or even "is this important?") before "how do I solve this?"

Why can also be applied to who; as in- who is the right person to tackle this challenge or chase this opportunity. So many leaders bottleneck themselves because they don't ask the right questions at the start line, and then find themselves in an unwinnable race.

Purpose Often Comes From Pain

Oprah Winfrey went through hell – on live television – when faced with the ramifications of a traumatic childhood. From this pain, she became no less than a gift to the world, helping others tell (if not embrace) their stories and help others cathartically heal through being vulnerable and sharing their pain and their triumphs.

Overcoming homelessness and addiction, it's no wonder my purpose is to expose people to – and lift them towards – their potential.

'Purpose' can seem an overwhelming concept, or it may lead people down a path of altruistic guilt if their purpose isn't to end poverty.

The fact is that there are many worthy causes in this world. The one that's touched your soul – is probably where you should start, with no justification or explanation. Just start helping!

Passion is a Window Into Purpose

Purpose can seem like an overwhelming concept for many. While there may be few bigger questions than why we are here, a great many of us also feel compelled by forces we don't even need to understand to create, experience, help, or learn in areas we just can't seem to get enough of.

It may not make practical sense right away in terms of building a career or generating revenue, but our passion is often the best place to look to gain wisdom into our calling. Even for those who aren't clear on their passion(s) yet, sound advice would be to follow their curiosity.

The questions we ask most often many times become the foundation of our passion which, given time and life experience, inform our life's purpose.

Values

Strategies are a Should; Values are a Must

A person without values is akin to a rudderless ship; doomed to ebb and flow to the demands of the waves (circumstances) pounding at its' hull.

Life is never short of demands to place on us; hence why the process of uncovering our unique set of core values is so important – our values truly are our moral compass.

If our strategy indicates our competence, then our values reveal our character!

Value is in the Eye of the Beholder

The great thing about uncovering your core values – is there is no wrong answer unless you half-ass the process.

For instance, my core value of "respect" (to me) means, "respect women, respect those who have been there before you, respect the elderly, respect Mother Nature, and earn respect rather than demand it". By comparison, I have seen others define the same value from what I would view as an entitled lens, uttering such comments as "don't you know who I am? Where is your respect?"

In the above example, the same value has drastically different meaning. There may be no right or wrong answer, the point is to find *your* definition to the values you live life by.

Everyone has Values

You tell yourself that you are speeding because you could be late for a meeting, and you don't want to disrespect the person you're about to meet with or devalue their time.

On the other hand, the person exhibiting the exact same driving behaviours that you are in the lane next to you is just an inconsiderate ass. See the irony?!

The fact is, we all view our own behaviours from the lens of our intention (our values). "I respect my client's precious time, so I must speed to be there on time". By contrast, we don't know a stranger's values, so we must infer them from their behaviour. ("They're speeding so they're obviously an impatient, inconsiderate jerk".)

Patience and understanding multiplies when we give others the benefit of the doubt!

Values Aren't Trendy, They're Timeless

The bad news for those who embrace core values like 'integrity' is that they may miss short term business opportunities like screwing others over to pursue short term profits. Doing the right thing is rarely cool, it's just respectable.

The good news is- short-term opportunists can rarely network past the pace of the relationships they ruin. Rock solid reliable will always come back in style, even if it isn't trendy at any given moment.

Staying true to you, and to your old school ethics will eventually become your advantage!

Values Bind More Than Opportunities

An accountant is always happy to outsource bookkeeping functions; until they hire a bookkeeper. Opportunities ebb and flow as business and markets evolve, and consumer behaviour inevitably changes.

That being said, two entrepreneurs who see eye to eye and can trust each other explicitly, will always find opportunities to support one another, and will find hesitation to take their business elsewhere.

Values endure far longer than opportunities born out of logic or convenience.

Mindset

Victor, not victim

Every day, in every situation, we are free to choose how we are to react to, then act upon, our circumstances. Even the toughest of challenges can present opportunities.

In my career I've coached a number of well-paid professionals who were laid off or let go for one reason or another. For many of them, once they got over the shock or fear, they embraced the fact that they actually hated the job they had, but were too afraid to try anything different. They could choose a "why me?" mentality, or they could choose to ask themselves "what now?" – and we have the same ability to choose my friends!

Embrace the Suck

Embrace the pain that separates you from your competition. Smile like you're getting away with something when you're up at 5am and working out while your competition sleeps – because you are!

When the road is hard, may you find fuel in the knowledge that the longer you toil, the more of your competitors have peeled away in search of easier paths.

Sometimes just not quitting is the difference between success and failure. If you have oxygen in your lungs and passion in your heart, you can always give your dreams at least one more try!

Live to Fight Another Day

Forgive yourself when you haven't conquered the world and accomplished everything on your list. Whether you are a student, employee, executive, or entrepreneur, there is always more we can be doing.

Learn how to say "enough is enough" and shut off so you can spend time with family and friends, or even alone recharging, so that you can tackle anew the opportunities and challenges that tomorrow will bring.

Rome wasn't built in a day; just like the masterpiece that will become your life will take time to manifest. Learn to work relentlessly each day, yet be patient when looking at the timelines your goals and dreams take to achieve.

Sacrifice is a Gift we Give Ourselves

In much of the world today, we live in a time of instant gratification and 'keeping up with the Jones's". We receive between 4,000 to 10,000 marketing impressions a day in North America – all designed to perpetuate an insatiable appetite for consumption and spending that feeds the corporate machine. As a result the majority of Canadians and Americans (as well as many other nations) spend more than they make.

By learning to work hard for delayed rewards, to learn to want less, and to be happy with what we have more than longing for what we don't – we can define happiness on our own terms. By embracing a long-term view of work vs reward, and by defining happiness through relationships and experiences more than belongings, we can create not only a more sustainable lifestyle, but also a more sustainable state of happiness.

The Beauty in Adversity

No one in their right mind asks for more adversity, failure, or roadblocks. That being said, we learn a lot more through failure or setbacks than we do through early success.

Just like the first mantra on page 22 suggests, if we can shift our mind from "why me?" to learn to seek the lessons our hardships are trying to teach us, we can turn the hardest moments in our lives into the best crucibles we have to forge our most valuable skills.

Think – what would you pay more for, a step-by-step explanation of $E=MC^2$, or advice from someone who's been there on how to get through your toughest challenges?

An ounce of wisdom is worth a pound of knowledge!

Be Above Your Thoughts

Notice negative thoughts, but don't let them land. Your thoughts are the precursor to your beliefs. Beliefs inform your emotions, and your emotions dictate your actions which produce your results. Don't let a negative thought take you all the way to a negative action, or a missed positive action. Notice your thoughts, and realize you don't need to own them!

For example: a "bad economy" (thought) can lead to a belief that a new business venture might be doomed to failure, resulting in an emotion of hopelessness, leading to inaction (not starting or trying to grow the business).

An entrepreneur with a different lens might see an opportunity (they might see a recession as one massive sale). That entrepreneur would take very different actions, and might enjoy much better results!

Bust Your Glass Ceiling

Notice the limitations embedded in your thoughts regarding your potential; learn to question why you limit how high you can go in your mind – because there is no threshold on success!

Any belief can be challenged and changed with evidence to the contrary. A married man who believes he is terrible at sales needs only to look at the ring on his finger to remind him he closed the biggest and most important sale of his life!

How and why do you hit a glass ceiling, and how can you change your thinking to change your potential?

Levelling up

There are times in our lives when we are called to a higher purpose. It could be our boss, our spouse, our goal, or the God (or Universe) we believe in telling us we were meant for more.

Four great ways to 'level up' are;

- Play on a better team (surround yourself with people who will stretch you in the areas you desire to grow)
- Hang with 10's (choose the crowd that demands you become a better version of yourself just to belong – while still remaining true to your core)
- Raise your standards (demand more of yourself as the minimum acceptable standard of behaviour, performance, or results)
- Lower the amount of BS you tolerate (this is your floor – the more you tolerate, the lower you sink. Be empathetic, but tolerate no anchors!)

Choose a Better State

Great news for anyone who wants more from life is that our mental and emotional state is not fixed. That is, we can choose how we feel, and that is like a superpower!

As page 27 outlines, our thoughts and beliefs happen before the emotions we experience. If we can learn to more accurately describe the emotions we are experiencing at any given time (for instance, "I'm feeling anxious" instead of "I'm stressed"), we give ourselves the power to reverse-engineer, and thus change, our state.

In the above example, you might question what is causing you anxiety, and you might pinpoint a looming event, or a person you're dealing with. Once we identify the source, or root cause of any emotion we wish to change, we can rise above our thinking (again page 27) and question, then challenge our feelings about anything!

The Riches are in the Niches

Less is more. Be great at one thing instead of trying to do everything. Our natural inclination is often to shore up our weaknesses, however the best we can hope for is to turn a weakness into a marginal competency, even after a lot of work. By doubling down on your strengths, you can turn them into potential areas of world class brilliance.

After all, how much would you pay Madonna to do your taxes? Probably a little bit less than you'd have to in order to hear her to sing!

Thinking is a Place

Find out where and when you do your best thinking. I used to walk my dog every afternoon as a chore so that I could work uninterrupted when I returned home. Now, the trails we hike every afternoon are where I gain most of my great ideas, and I never have a 2, 3, or 4pm crash! For others, it might be sitting on a park bench enjoying the view. For my mentor, it's at his lake cabin, atop a remote cliff-diving site where he can overlook most of the beautiful lake and inspire "blue sky view, no limits ideas".

Our brain has several different functions, and with them – different modes of thinking. We often do our best creative thinking after we exhaust the task-oriented centers of our brain. Knowing when and where you do your best thinking helps you avoid trying to fit a square peg in a round hole when it comes to how your brain works.

It's hard for your brain to answer the "what's my purpose?" types of questions when it is in a task-oriented or computing "what's 2 + 2?" state.

You wouldn't book an important business meeting to go over financials at a rock concert, so why ask your brain and heart to answer your most compelling 'why?' questions when you have 5 minutes in between meetings while sitting in front of your computer?

Discipline is the Unsexiest Secret to Success

Hard work is rarely sexy. Neither is discipline, sacrifice, minimalism, or delayed gratification. It seems that many young people today have aspirations of greater success than the generation before them, with hopes of a faster pathway to get there, requiring less effort.

While improvements in technology and the advent of the internet and social media have allowed many tech savvy entrepreneurs to build successful enterprises seemingly overnight, the fact is for most people success takes time.

More importantly, success takes a lot of sacrifice. Money, parties, luxury items and often sleep must be exchanged for long hours studying, working, researching, and honing your craft.

Shortcuts are rarely born out of laziness, though that is the attempt. In most cases, as unsexy as it may sound, the fastest way to leapfrog others on the way to attaining your goals is to stay more focused, more disciplined, and to work harder than others who aspire to the same level of success as you do.

Disciplined, hard work may not be sexy, but it never goes out of style.

The sacrifices and extra effort you put in through the building years of your career (or relationship or in training as an athlete) yield the results that the less disciplined can only dream of in the end!

Success is Not the Absence of Problems

Everyone has problems. One of the biggest mistakes I see people make in my coaching practice is that when I ask people for their goals, they envision an unattainable future. That is, they dream of a better future that's impossible to achieve because they dream of happily ever after.

Oprah Winfrey can't go out in public without being mobbed for autographs. That's still a problem. The greatest problem in business is when demand outpaces supply; you just can't build it fast enough. Great problem to have, but it's still a problem.

Don't confuse challenges for failure. We all have problems, and even if yours seem paralyzing at the moment, it doesn't mean you're not already a success. Now go manifest better problems!

No Plan B

Just as Captain Hernán Cortés ordered his men to burn their boats upon arriving in Veracruz in 1519, your Plan B must be scrapped if Plan A is to have no choice but success.

Even if no physical time or energy is expended, the very existence of a 'Plan B' detracts from Plan A. First, most noteworthy goals entail a fair amount of hard work, even struggle, en route to their attainment. Having an exit strategy allows you a mental off-ramp if the going gets too tough.

Second, when success is your only option, there is a level of creativity that flows from desperation that just can't be reached when you are operating from a relative comfort zone.

When success is your only option, all potential strategies are focused on one thing, instead of being spread across multiple possibilities, where opportunity cost can paralyze action.

Attitude Before Aptitude

In my second business, I had to fire two fitness professionals with masters degrees (many personal trainers have a high school education and aren't even certified). The first human resources director we hired had an absolutely brilliant resume, but was so harsh with people we had to let them go. And then we had to demote a member of our executive team with an MBA from Harvard.

There are exceptions to every rule, but in my 22 years of business, when you hire the resume, you often have to fire the person. When you hire for attitude – surprise – driven people are hungry to learn and the resume gets better over time.

This must start with the leader (you) first and foremost. The attitude a leader brings to their team (caring, supportive, accountable, high standards, etc) is more important than the management tools. Great teams start there.

Failure is Part of the Journey

Any true success has probably faced more failure than their counterparts. Put another way, they've had more strikeouts, but in large part this is because they've stepped up to bat so many times. Thomas Edison put it aptly when he said, "I have not failed. I've just found 10,000 ways that won't work".

Michael Jordan, the best basketball player of all time, said it best. "I've missed more than 9,000 shots in my career. I've lost almost 300 games. Twenty-six times, I've been trusted to take the game winning shot and missed. I've failed over and over and over again in my life. And that is why I succeed."

As unattractive a formula as it may be, failure is an essential part of the learning process. Learning is the cornerstone of success because what is success other than the product of *effort, talent and attitude combined with strategy towards a meaningful goal*?

Habits

Where Habits Start

Great habits don't start when your feet hit the floor – they start the night before! Getting your clothes ready for the next day = one less decision you need to waste cognitive function on (and you save time); and getting your workout attire laid out where you can't miss it = no missed workouts. What you *act* on with consistency matters far more than the quality of your intentions.

If our actions are taken to achieve desired results, then our habits should be focused, repeated actions centered around our most important desired outcomes!

Ask – are your habits a function of autopilot, or of careful intention?

Morning routine

The key to a GREAT day is to begin your day with...

- Gratitude: a deep sense of what you appreciate and are thankful for. Don't just write a list – think about who and what you appreciate until you reach a truly blessed state. The fact is your heart can't fit gratitude and fear (or anger) in the same place at the same time.
- Relationships: reflect each day, even briefly, on the state of your important relationships, and what you can do to improve them, or to honor those you love
- Exercise: move your body every morning. Lift weights, run, take a class, do yoga, even just stretching sore muscles will improve health, brain function, and mood, among a plethora

of other health benefits (like having the energy to maintain a hectic schedule)
- Achieve: visualize every meeting, and every important task you're about to embark on for the day. Now imagine everything goes amazingly. You landed the big contract, you aced your presentation, and you finished that important report on time.
- Tweak: if you reflected on 13 big ticket items for your day, is it realistic that they all end up as home runs? On the other hand, do you only have two items on your list that you can finish by noon? Tweak your to do list accordingly so that you can accomplish much, but not set yourself up for failure by taking on too much (or too little).

Everything has a Place

How much time have you wasted in your life looking for your keys, phone, or wallet? Rather than coming home and dropping everything at the front door (or scattered as you make your way through your house or apartment), have a consistent, never-changes place for these items you always need (and that are often misplaced).

Not only can this simple act save you minutes every single week (time is money) but more importantly it saves throwing you off emotionally before a big meeting, or making you late for one.

Small, disciplined mental habits play a big role in how successful someone ultimately becomes.

Scoreboard for Success

We all need a scoreboard for success. The fact is success means different things to different people. Perhaps your definition of success is the amount of time spent with your kids every day during the week. Perhaps it's how many others you can help every day. Perhaps it's a financial nest egg that will allow you to retire. Whatever it is, be sure to get crystal clear on how you define, and measure success, and then monitor your success metrics daily (or as frequently as appropriate) because what gets measured becomes what gets accomplished.

My favorite success metric is S.T.A.W. I always explain to entrepreneurs that the best way to build a business is brick by brick, through a solid foundation of consistent, practical fundamentals. That being said, while you execute the little things day in and day out, step up to the plate and take a few home run swings every now and then! S.T.A.W. for me stands for shit thrown against the wall – and if I try something crazy every single week, even if it only works 1% of the time, then on average I will experience a life-changing breakthrough every two years! That's how I got published in Entrepreneur magazine, and that's how I got onto most of the stages I've spoken from!

Get smarter during your commute.

Why listen to the same music every time you get in your car? Unless you are a new driver, your commute is the perfect time for passive learning.

Listening to audiobooks or podcasts allows you to multitask in a way that doesn't distract. Apps like Blinkist or Read it For Me can even condense books into their key points so that you can fast-track your learning and just read the full versions of the books that resonate the most with you.

Why not arrive to every meeting smarter than you were than when you left your house?

Personal Betterment Isn't a One-off

As challenging as it may be to make the decision, then balance your priorities as you commit to continuing education or other forms of personal growth, it just doesn't work as a 'one-off'.

The fact is, you're either growing as a person each and every day, or you are becoming more and more complacent. Even the highest of achievers have complacent days, but they are the exception, and just about all of the world-changers you'll ever read about make up for what they consider a 'lazy day' (usually for several days after).

For these reasons, personal betterment is more of a process, and a habit, than it is a course or even a phase. Remember – our results dictate our actions, and our habits can be viewed as the actions we take most often. Personal growth, when it really works, is more like a way of life than it is a period of our lives.

Goal Setting

The Importance of Goals

Zig Ziglar, in his "Goal Setting Guide" discusses the true value of goals. To Ziglar, the inherent value of setting goals is not in achieving them, but rather in the kind of person they make you become in order to achieve your goals.

All that really matters – is that your goals matter to you. If your goal matters, actions will follow and you will be stretched as a person and a professional. Keep this process going over a lifetime, and it becomes profound not only what you'll achieve, but who you'll become!

Start NOW!

Call it a list of 'Goals Before I Die'; because you will. Why wait until your doctor tells you that you've got six months to live to start *living*?!

I ask people all the time – if you were told you had six months to live, what would you change? The only thing that should truly change is our spending habits, because we no longer need to be saving for retirement.

If you were going to start skydiving, hiking, seeing your best friends more often, and writing a book or a song because you suddenly realize you're going to die – do those things now!

Start your list, and include goals from every important area of your life (business, health, relationships, wealth, travel, philanthropy, learning, etc) and include some that are just for fun!

We All Need Stretch Goals

Set goals that scare and excite you at the same time. A good stretch goal is like a 'why' without the 'how'. In other words, it gives your heart permission to give a voice to your biggest dreams without the potentially cynical part of your brain ruining them by debating the likelihood of their achievement.

Resonance, or how much a goal matters to you, is far more important than how realistic its' achievement may be.

If your heart and soul command you to land on the moon, your brain will figure out how to build a rocket ship.

Goals Perpetuate Progress

For many people, a 'to do list' becomes little more than an overgrown list of chores. If we can learn instead to embrace the scoreboard for success concept (page 45), we can break down our major success measures into short-term bite-size chunk measurables. From here, we can set short term goals that hold us accountable to daily and weekly action that, added up over time, fuels progress and achievement.

A to do list can weigh us down over time, bearing little more than a sense of obligation. Daily and weekly goals around the quality and quantity of our input (effort) can make all the difference in the world!

Effectiveness

Time ~~Management~~ *Maximization*

Leadership expert John Maxwell talks about how we can't manage time (there will always be 24 hours in a day and 7 days in a week), so we must instead manage our priorities. I tend to agree, and a few ways we can manage our priorities are;

- Planning our weeks in advance (for example, plan the week ahead on Thursday afternoon)
- Reviewing each day at night, assessing productivity based on your goals and tweaking the next day based on output
- Blocking time (email from 2-3pm or prospecting for new business @ 8 – 11)
- Take a break every ~90 minutes to stay productive!
- Planning for the year ahead in late November/ early December
- When planning above, include health, business, relationship, financial, and other priorities to ensure balance
- Review your plan every month

Don't Leave the Seminar with Good Intentions

Act in the moment of inspiration, don't add it to your to do list for when you get back to your desk (when you're sure to be in a different state).

So often after a great meeting, inspiring speaker, or even a great TED talk we mentally commit to a new behavior or a committed action, and then we go back to our busy life and – do nothing.

Do something that commits you to the change you wanted to make right in the moment of inspiration or we don't create momentum for ourselves to enable the changes we hope to make.

Success Leaves Clues

Chances are, no matter how audacious or specific your goals may be, someone has achieved a similar level of success as you aspire to. Find mentors who have walked the path you hope to, and reach out to them. It could be the Chief Marketing Officer within your organization, the couple who just celebrated 50 years of marriage who are still in love, or it may be the worlds' foremost expert in your field.

I have three mentors I've never even met, but I've read five of their books, as well as read or watched countless articles, interviews, and other online content they've produced.

As my chief mentor often says, "the formula for success need not be reinvented, it just needs to be implemented". Watch, learn, then do what those whose success you hope to emulate have done.

The Untapped Goldmine Next Door

Every lifelong friend you have, and every brand new connection you make, are just waiting to help you make your dreams a reality. It may be an introduction to their uncle who's looking to hire someone just like you, or it could be your accountant who would be more than happy to refer you a steady stream of new clients.

Only two things stand in the way of your network going to work hard for you. First off, the knowledge of how they can help you. This is why 12 connections you meet with on a somewhat regular basis are more powerful than 1000 followers on any social media channel. If your network knows what you're passionate about, skilled at, and looking to attract to yourself, they are armed to go to work for you rather than just like your posts.

Second, if your network feels indebted to you because you are always looking to serve and support others, you begin to amass a community of others dedicated to helping you in return.

This is not to advise helping others for the sole purpose of gaining favors in return. Help others because it's the right thing to do, and you will feel great for doing it. The fact that those who you can help will want to help you too is simply an amazing bonus!

The abundance you create for others begets the abundance you will attract into your own life, it's that simple.

Follow up and Follow Through

Two of the most important keys to becoming more effective are to stay on top of your commitments, and to see them through. Whether you keep a log of your outstanding items, or you write "follow up with Susan" as an appointment next Tuesday in your calendar, it is imperative to success for busy people to a) have a method of keeping on top of all of their commitments and b) finding a method other than short term memory.

Treat your word like a contract. If you say you're going to do something, find a way, no matter the circumstances, of getting it done. You won't be remembered for your intentions; you'll be remembered for your actions. Better make sure your actions match your promises.

Don't Compare Your Life to the Highlight Reel

If we wish to remain highly effective each day (if not each hour), then it is of critical importance that we feed our mind and spirit positive, high quality inputs.

While goal setting is essential (pages 49-53), it's also crucial to set your own scoreboard for success (page 45). One of the worst scoreboards for success – is other people's social media feeds.

There are two reasons not to compare yourself to others on social media. First, it's misrepresentative. Do you post every time you're having a bad day? Do you post every time you perform a mundane task? Do you post when you get nothing but bills in the mail? No. Most people post only their brightest moments like holidays, meeting their idols, getting the new job or work promotions, hence the term 'highlight reel'.

The second reason not to compare to the highlight reel is there is no context. You might be struggling for six weeks with a challenge, only to scroll social media and see someone is crushing it at work doing exactly what you are trying to. You might instantly feel inadequate, depressed, or like a failure, but you have no way of knowing that the highlight that just depressed you came after 12 weeks of struggling. You might be further ahead than the person you're jealous of, but you just lack the context to know it!

Social media has many benefits, but it has many harmful side effects if we don't exercise some mental discipline as we consume online content.

Run your own race, at your own pace, and you'll realize you have no reason to compare yourself to others anyway!

Health

It's Too Nice to be Inside!

If, like me, you grew up in the 1970's or 80's (or before) you can probably remember your parents uttering this exact phrase every weekend and every summer. The fact is, getting outside every day provides a plethora of health benefits, and also improves cognitive function.

Walking away from your computer when you feel like you're blankly staring at the screen, then taking a walk in nature, changes your mental state from intense conscious focus to subconscious wandering. Ironically, this is often when we form new mental connections. In other words, we often ask the question at our desk, but receive the answer in our garden!

If nothing else, fresh air and physical activity feels good, improves your mood, and will help you live longer – there's a reason Einstein took a nice long walk every day!

Don't Exercise; Train

Most people view exercise as a chore, some even as a punishment. "I have to exercise tomorrow because there were donuts in the lunch room today and I ate three!"

Rather than being the hardest task in your day, whose sole purpose is to shed calories and stave off Father Time, learn to view exercise as an opportunity. Athletes train to prepare themselves for competition. Why can't professionals view their performances as needing just as serious a set of preparatory disciplines?

Instead of reluctantly exercising to work off a beer gut, try embracing exercise as training to give you the energy to outwork your peers and be able to play with your kids?

Instead of preventing osteoporosis, exercise could be preparing you for the massive presentation or busy season at work!

Exercise Also Builds Your Resiliency Muscle

You probably already know that the health benefits of exercise are plentiful, and multi-faceted. You probably also know that regular exercise will give you the energy reserves you'll need to pursue your most important pursuits, whether it's a career in music or playing golf professionally.

No doubt you're aware that there are bound to be roadblocks on any important journey – but did you know exercise helps make you more resilient in the face of adversity? By routinely pushing yourself through challenging workouts, and remaining committed to exercise even on days when you don't feel like it, you're building the resiliency you'll need to weather challenges. You could face financial hardship, relationship strain, mis-starts, tough feedback, failure, or all of the above en route to building your dream. If you can muster that 20th push-up or run that 5th mile, you can overcome your other challenges!

You DO Have the Time and Equipment to Get Fit

Where there's a will there's a way. Everyone is busy, but no one should be so busy they don't have time for a life or to improve themselves.

Even if you have no equipment, commitment and creativity can go a long way. Completing as many burpees as you can in 7 minutes goes beyond 'effective' as a workout and lives clearly in the category of workouts I never want to do again!

Jumping jacks, shadow boxing, marching, running, stair repeats, planks, push ups and more can all be completed in an apartment, a hotel room, or just about any room for that matter.

If exercise (or anything else) matters, it will ascend your priority list and replace TV, a few minutes of sleep, or scrolling social media. Or, it won't and you can be just like everybody else. Your choice.

Food is Either Medicine or Poison

There's an old saying in fitness circles that "abs are made in the kitchen". I would argue that sustained energy, mood, mental clarity, disposition, immunity, and vitality are also made in the kitchen. Depending on what's in the fridge and pantry, sickness and a host of other unwelcome conditions also come from the kitchen.

Of course people who eat extremely healthy food can still get sick, but on the whole – our bodies are just like the cars we drive. You wouldn't put low quality fuel in a sports car, and you wouldn't head out on a road trip with an empty gas tank, would you?

There's always a place for your favorite treats or snacks, but most people can benefit from being far more conscious of what they put in their mouths.

Relationships

Take Stock Every Day

Life moves fast. Anyone with children in their lives knows that. Having finished this book on a trip to Greece, the 11 years that have passed since my wife and I were married there seemed to have flown by. Then again, on this trip to see my wife's dad again, we were also bringing along a ten year old!

More gravely, I'm a heart attack survivor. You never know when your time is up, so every day while you make to do lists, take stock of the important relationships in your life, and ask yourself how you're showing up; and whether you're pulling your weight in each of those relationships.

All relationships take work, and that work needs to happen regularly, not 'when you have time'.

Let Them Know in Real Time

If you live long enough, you're going to lose people you love. I've had the opportunity to tell four close loved ones how much they meant to me on their deathbeds before they passed. As tough as those moments were, they also were extraordinarily meaningful. That made me think – "why on Earth am I waiting until these people die to have these conversations?!"

Some of the best conversations I've ever had were when I told my parents, my best friends, my mentors, and my wife and son what they meant to me – on a Tuesday instead of when they were facing terminal illness.

Let your loved ones know in real time how much they mean to you, and watch your relationships take on a whole new life!

You're Showing People How to Treat You

If you've read this book in order, and you've uncovered your core values discussed in the second section of this book, you've already met others who share a very different world view. From the lens of core values, even right and wrong are not universal concepts.

On the one hand, what a world it would be if everyone shared high-minded ideals of kindness, generosity, empathy, and helping others. On the other hand, if everyone was the same, how boring would life be?

Even when you come into conflict with others who seem to be downright awful, it's important to master our own emotional state, words, and actions. The Holy Bible teaches us to "turn the other cheek" when we are offended or attacked. I agree with the spirit of these teachings, but I also believe in standing up for what's right.

As a coach who studies human psychology, I also believe that we are always learning at the subconscious, if not conscious level.

When someone is rude or completely offside in their treatment of us (or others) and we do nothing, we are (through our inaction) teaching them that there is no consequence to their misbehaviour and so by being complicit, we are in a way teaching them that how they are behaving is ok.

While I am in no way condoning violence or vengeance as a reaction, there are many ways our words or actions can send a different message that when others offend us, it is not okay and we will not tolerate it.

As "leveling up" suggests (page 29), raising our standards is one major way to change our reality, including how others treat us. Set high standards for how you treat yourself, and how you teach others to treat you.

Be the Example

As mentioned on page 70, all relationships take work. Sometimes, in our closest relationships with family or friends, we feel wronged and can become deeply hurt.

'Stonewalling' is a common defense mechanism that shows up during conflict in relationships (think 'cold shoulder'). Stonewalling provides an effective mental analogy, because the longer we avoid our loved ones, the taller and more insurmountable the wall becomes.

Erma Bombeck wrote "a child needs your love most when he deserves it least". I don't think a spouse or any other loved one is any different.

If we can let go of our wounded pride (without compromising our dignity or values), we can recall the perspective of what kind of relationship we'd ideally like to have. From this perspective, we usually treat others much differently than from our wounded, resentful state.

So long as you are not ignoring the signs of an unhealthy or abusive relationship, learn to let go of the childish, selfish ego who wants revenge. Instead, strive always to be the example of how to treat each other, and of the respectful, loving, blissful relationships you'd love to cultivate in your life.

Be the example!

Paying it Forward

We all Have Something to Give

Many people mistake 'giving back' as something to do after they've 'made it'. The fact is you don't need to be wealthy, or a world class expert in order to be of service to others.

We all have time, even in the building years of our career or when our kids are young. Even one hour a week, compounded over time, can make a huge difference in the lives of others.

Everyone also has a talent. You might donate your creative services for a not-for-profit, perform basic accounting services for a charity for free, or spend time with seniors every week in a retirement home just listening.

Finally, our wealth comes in many forms. If you don't have money to donate right now, you still might have old clothes, old toys, or even old furniture to donate to a women's shelter, Goodwill, or many other charitable causes. We all have something to give!

The Best Way to Learn is to Teach

Reading articles and books or listening to podcasts or lectures lead to acquiring new knowledge. Having to do it yourself leads to a much more thorough practical understanding. When we teach others what we've learned however, we begin to understand our newly acquired wisdom in much deeper ways, and from multiple perspectives.

David Sandler said it best in his book, "You Can't Learn to Ride a Bike at a Seminar"!

Make a point of helping and teaching others as you continue to learn, and you'll benefit through the process too. Students who don't become teachers in some way are doomed to forget much of what they've learned.

Wisdom is a Terrible Secret Weapon

Continued education is one of the fastest ways anyone can improve their inherent value. That being said, the value of your specific knowledge base is directly related to the severity of problems you can solve for others, and how many such people you can help.

For these reasons, withholding expertise in hopes of upselling, or trying to monetize 'informational asymmetry' (when the general public has limited access to key information experts possess), ultimately limits your earning potential.

The more people you can help, and the greater degree to which you can help them, the better off you (and those you help) will be.

Achievements Lead to a Living, Altruism Leads to Your Legacy

In order to succeed in any career (or any endeavour for that matter), one must work very hard, as well as acquire the necessary experience, expertise, and credentials that will help gain the trust of customers (or their bosses), and separate themselves from their competition. While hard work, skills, knowledge, and an impressive resume may lead to career and financial success, many professionals who attain this level of success are left wanting more.

As hard as some people find attaining this level of success to be, it may be all for naught if we come to the realization that our life lacks significance. This does not mean some of our career milestones don't matter – they do indeed. What the most successful people on the planet come to understand is that true significance – the mark of a truly extraordinary life – comes from the service of others.

No one will remember your grade point average after you've left high school or university, and even if it made millionaires of your teammates, few people will remember landing the Johnson deal at your retirement party.

The small, selfless acts of service for others however, define how people feel about you, and how they describe you. Would people be more likely to describe their friend Jennifer as a professional engineer, or the kindest person they've ever met?

Truly holistic success is a balance between achievement and altruism. What you can achieve will likely pay the mortgage, but what you give becomes a far more valuable currency in the hearts and minds of others!

EPILOGUE:

SUCCESS IS A SYSTEM

If you've learned anything from this book, I hope you will learn its final lesson. To this end, I suggest that success is a system, and its component parts are transferrable across disciplines. The fundamentals required to become a successful athlete are the same required to succeed in business, relationships, or philanthropy.

After studying the works of Zig Ziglar, Tony Robbins, John Maxwell, Ken Blanchard, Robin Sharma, Dr. Marshall Goldsmith, John Mattone, Dale Carnegie, Napoleon Hill, and so many others, as well as interviewing some of the most successful leaders in the world today (for my 5th book, stay tuned!), the patterns become transparently clear.

If success is a system, then this author would argue its component parts can be organized into 10 simple steps as follows;

1. Identify a clear purpose that is larger than yourself and compelling enough to

drive action on days you otherwise wouldn't feel like it.
2. Through introspection, uncover your own unique set of core values that act as your moral compass in how you make all of the important decisions in your life.
3. Understand that the mind is our most powerful tool, and that we are in control of our thoughts in any situation. Through this knowledge, we can choose to raise our standards and demand higher quality thoughts. Do so ASAP!
4. Knowing that our thoughts inform our beliefs, build a set of beliefs about yourself, the world, and others that is aligned with the highest quality of life you aspire to.
5. Set goals in all important areas of life, from wealth to health and from relationships to responsibilities. Those goals should range from immediate

term (this week) to bucket list (before I die), but they should all matter to you.
6. Once goals are set, rigid yet adaptable plans must be constructed for their attainment.
7. Regular, if not daily reflection of these goals needs to become a habit.
8. Implementing daily routines designed to optimize your mindset, health, and emotional state becomes critical in maximizing your effectiveness and moving closer to the attainment of your goals and becoming the best version of yourself.
9. Surrounding yourself with mentors and those who challenge you to be better is just as important as spending time with those who love you just the way you are.
10. As we go on to manifest lives that are the stuff of legend, we must always remember that we needed and benefited from help along the way. No

definition of success is complete without giving back, and so it becomes our duty to help others who have no clear way of paying us back. Through achievement we find success; through helping others we find significance.

It is a profound professional joy to give back to you, dear reader, and share what I have learned (so far) in hopes that you may build a life that matches your scoreboard for success.

To your success, and to those lives you will go on to improve,

Stan

About the Author

Success is a System is Stan Peake's fourth book. Besides being a bestselling author (How to Sell in Any Economy went # 1 in 3 categories on Amazon in 2018), Stan is also a master certified executive coach, keynote speaker & corporate facilitator. He is the founder of InSite Performance Coaching.

Stan has coached and worked with owners and executives in some of the world's largest companies, and has also coached over 100 of the next wave of entrepreneurs & leaders from all over Canada, the United States, and Europe.

When not coaching, speaking, or writing, Stan loves spending time with his wife Maria, son Chase, and dog Zeke. Together they enjoy travelling, going to the movies, and staying active wherever they go.

Stan can be found on LinkedIn or reached at stan@insiteperformancecoaching.com

Made in the
USA
Middletown, DE